Bold, intimate, and profoundly human, *Troublemaker* is a collection that doesn't just speak, it resonates long after the final page is turned."

Stephanie Lamb
Editor-in-Chief, Quillkeepers Press

Bold, intimate, and profoundly human, *Troublemaker* is a collection that doesn't just speak, it resonates long after the final page is turned."

PRAISE FOR *TROUBLEMAKER*

"*Troublemaker* is a collection that keeps you on your toes. Challenging the idea of being a 'good girl,' Laura Van Vorst's poems encourage us to be braver, bigger and more self-aware. This is a book that is full of grief, hope, love, friendship and joy, and most of all makes me want to skip into the light holding the label of 'too much' like a messy bouquet ready to be thrown out with power and with pride. I hold these poems like a secret note of self-assurance… This carefully crafted collection of poems is a battle cry, a spring in your step, and a gut punch that stings your teeth but leaves you giddy with the sugar rush of knowing yourself. I love these poems."

Laurie Bolger

Award-winning poet, founder of *The Creative Writing Breakfast Club*, and author of *Lady*.

"Laura's poems haven't been written; they've been earned. Like the 'stretch marks' she writes of, these pieces bear witness to the growth that emerges through belief and doubt, grief and longing, asking and seeking, waiting and wandering. I felt the aching shadow of her father's passing, the primal force of labour and birth, the depth of a partner's love spanning big changes, and the liberating taste of more expansive beliefs taking root where old ones have passed away. It's a privilege to sit with these intimate and evocative portraits of a life moving through shifting seasons, like a garden wilting and blooming and coming alive, again and again."

Will Small

3X Australian Poetry Slam National Finalist, author of *Poems for When the World is Ending* and founding director of Lead by Story.

"Laura Van Vorst's *Troublemaker* is a rich, lyrical journey that carries the reader through faith, love, grief, womanhood, and the natural world with stunning precision and heart. Her bold, inquisitive voice leaves no aspect of the human experience untouched. Vulnerable, elegant, and inventive in form, this collection is a radiant and powerful treasure."

Naomi Anne Goldner
Writer and Editor-in-Chief, Chariot Press Literary Journal

"*Troublemaker* is a luminous and gut-honest exploration of what it means to question, grieve, love, and grow in the wild terrain of being human. With equal parts fire and tenderness, Laura Van Vorst traces the shifting seasons of a life, moving from the upheaval of rethinking long-held beliefs to the cold ache of loss, and into the warm, unruly bloom of love, friendship, and self-acceptance.

Across four vivid sections: *Troublemaker*, *Ghost*, *Lover*, and *Wildflower*, Van Vorst's poems crackle with sharp wit, lyrical beauty, and a stunning emotional clarity. She writes about faith that sheds its leaves, grief that lingers like a second skin, the raw honesty of motherhood, and the quiet rebellions that make us whole again. Her voice is unflinching yet generous, inviting readers to see themselves in the cracks, the questions, the tenderness, and the transformation.

Perfect for readers who have ever wondered if they were "too much," who have survived the dark and reached for the light, and who understand that becoming oneself is both an unravelling and a blooming.

TROUBLEMAKER

Cover design by Laura Van Vorst and Bethany Nixon.

Cover image: 'Trespassing' 2025 © Bethany Tara Photography.

Tree illustrations by Laura Van Vorst.

Wildflower illustrations by a friend, with gratitude for their artistry.

Published by Innogen Press. Sydney, Australia.

ISBN 978-1-7643755-0-4

eISBN 978-1-7643755-1-1

TROUBLEMAKER

(and other self-portraits)

Laura Van Vorst

INNOGEN

for Joshua, who sees every version of me
and loves me in every season,
no matter how wild I grow

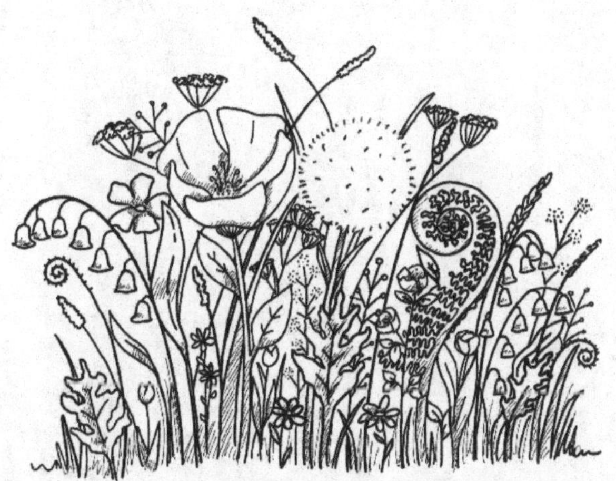

PROLOGUE

I never meant to be a troublemaker.

This collection of poems explores questions about faith, trauma and grief, identity in motherhood, loss and growth. These are the hard things to talk about, and can be so unwelcome in polite conversation, but when someone is brave enough to be honest about them, I've learned that as the tell; those are my people.

Sometimes it feels like being open about these things makes me an accidental troublemaker – *why can't you just trust? stay the same? keep quiet? loosen up?* – and maybe that's because I grew up so invested in being a 'good girl', amenable and studious. One autumn I started questioning everything, and in the coming seasons I moved from being a troublemaker to a ghost, a lover, a wildflower. Perhaps you have moved through these seasons too.

If you're naturally compliant like me, you'll probably read these poems in the order I've chosen. But if you're keen to venture off-track, here's a roadmap that might be helpful: For poems that wrestle with questions and changing beliefs, start at the beginning with *Troublemaker*. This section focuses on my experience of rethinking the belief system I grew up in. For poems about the cold, dark moments in life, and how these experiences co-create us, you'll want *Ghost*. These poems are about losing my dad when I was thirteen, and how that coloured everything that came after. They explore the ways we allow ourselves to become invisible, and the impact that has on a person's sense of self.

You'll find poems about the hope that blossoms out of love and friendship in the third section, *Lover*. These are my love letters to my people, who have sat in the messy, authentic, impolite moments with me. It turns out it's our relationships that save us, in the end. The last section, *Wildflower*, is about summer, growth, and self-acceptance. May we all remember that we are a part of the wild world, with just as much right to grow wherever we find ourselves.

If you've ever wondered if you are "too much," if you've ever disappeared into a traumatic moment, if you are overcome with gratitude for your people, if you're ready to embrace your wildness and worthiness – then I hope you'll find yourself reflected here. Maybe together we'll stop being scared to make trouble and use that fire to make the world better. We'll grow through the wild summer, ready to watch the leaves crisp and fall again, like they always do.

Content note: Some of these poems discuss gendered violence, political violence, pregnancy, birth stories, harmful religious theology, death and grief. Please take care while reading.

I

Wash injustice out to sea.
Mover? Shaker?
Troublemaker.

I Tend

to skip right to the end
so this floundering and wandering is new
but necessary.

I tend
I tend
I tend
yet a field of wildflowers needs no tending.

A baby cries in the night
her bedroom deep like a forest
but Mum is just three paces down the hall
closing space with every step.

The closets are empty of monsters.
So settle in, my darling.
We will find the light
by resting in the darkness first.

Lost

I used to take the long way home
crisscrossing streets to unfamiliar
just enough to find
trees I did not recognise
shedding leaves like dropping breadcrumbs.
I'd press on
so close to home
but dying to get lost
and found again.

And now I find myself on long walks over dunes of sand
upturning stones to look for treasure
clutching pebbles in worn hands
cold fingers testing shapes
keeping prizes in a pocket
finding stones already hid there
discarding ones that do not fit

choosing what to keep
and what to leave;
dying to get lost
and found again.

But just like when oceans
push rough to smooth,
massaging hands
press knot to bruise,
these falling rocks
are painful to lose

and on dry paths
leaves shrivel, fall
and shatter underfoot.

Uninvited

I'm scared to speak my doubts
or pose my questions
uninvited
I might shift the ground beneath you

expose the gaps
I've fallen into
drag you in unwilling too

tripping over potholes;
at first it looked like one or two
with sure terrain between
till eyes accustomed to the dark
spot more and more, like stars appearing
across swelling sky
stretched out below like dark velvet
the solid ground now high above
and out of reach;
turned upside down, I'm not sure
if I'm broken or just giddy
with the possibilities

so I'll stand with dizzy smile
pretend I'm still upright while my heart drops, bounces, shatters
and the endless quilt below
draws close and warm and then slips far away
my legs wobble on a balance beam
eyes strain through inky dark

my standstill a wordless reminder:
for God's sake
don't
look
down.

I Never Knew Faith Was So Deciduous.

The air   smells   different
this summer; some days
light and heat
beam down until I bloom like a sunflower,
tall as the backyard fence. Some days
I don't realise the scorch
until red spreads over skin.

Next day, wild wintry winds
whip hair around faces
Sheets of rain
wash away plans.
Darkened receipts of summer
and certainty
turn brittle and useless
fall to the ground
like silent angels.

I swear the sunlight is shortening.

Some days hold still and cold
stark
as empty branches
waiting
for budburst.

VOICE

I spent years with my head covered and bowed
before pulpits populated by powerful men
painting God in their image.

My voice was a sin.

What I would have given
for a sermon that rendered God's heart full,
blended in the brushstrokes of a mother –
just once, to have heard the echoes of the Marys
entrusted with the Gospel. I longed
for the truth: Spirit didn't ask me
to deny that I was angry,
for she was angry too.

These bones and brains and beating heart
were sculpted into a main event,
not shaped to be a support act, silent in a pew.

My voice was a hidden offence

but I found it pressed between Bible pages
concealed in the folds of my Sunday dress
passed between friends like secret notes in the back row.

It was years before I stepped outside
and words began to rumble in my belly
just echoes at first
resonance of women I saw on stages
mirrors with microphones

volcanoes erupting, crescendo.

I felt the pressure build –
I couldn't keep my mouth shut any longer.
A tentative throat-clearing, shaky whisper, *Testing 1– 2–*
an improvised bridge building to chorus
harmony / discord.

Now I look straight ahead
my curls exploding like flames;
I paint these pages bright,
    bellow till I'm winded,
        crash through buildings,
           start a thunderstorm
                lightning bolt spotlight
                [one Mississippi]
                booming lament
                cloud smash
                battle cry.

Good Friday Agreement

Before the people of Northern Ireland
voted *yes* with t r e m b l i n g hands,
embraced the resurrection of a country
known for its bombs and not its beauty,
its conflict and not its character,

before we built a causeway over ensanguined land

I had seen my Granda checking under his car every morning
for bombs planted by those
who hoped he wouldn't make it to work.

I had walked through the doors of shopping centres
offering my Hello Kitty backpack for review
not on exit,
for they weren't concerned about what a seven-year-old would
steal
but on entry
for they feared what an adult might have planted
to explode on a supermarket shelf.

I had heard the commotion
of pulling the alarm for an abandoned rucksack, suspicious in
library stacks.

I had heard the thump
        thump
        thump of a Lambeg drum
        that claimed to celebrate victory
        but only ever made me frightened;
I had been asked at school
if I were *Protestant* or *Catholic*.
I had known the answer,
but not why it mattered.

I don't remember if it rained or shined the day we voted yes
but I remember the sunshine we pinned to our lapels
the smell of smoke replaced by the smell of hope
the taste of fear still fresh on our tongues
the red ribbons plaited through my hair.

I remember the spring in our steps
the new life pressing into blossom
the blood that poured from violent hearts
run dry and buried
the stone rolled away –

The ending. The beginning.

Red Ribbon

In my earliest memory
I am five years old, peering through the living room window
at a removal van
pulled up next door.
Two girls with red-ribboned pigtails
three boys tall and lanky
a father with a wide smile
a mother with a long plait and rounded belly
unloading boxes
carrying lamps and statues and mismatched chairs.

My grandmother frowns over my shoulder
mutters to my father
about the area
      going
      downhill.

We know,
although they never say so;
it's the ornaments they display in windows
their five-times-handed-down dungarees
the edges of their consonants
the names I've never heard.
I am one of three in my class;
I roll their unfamiliar syllables around on my tongue.

The children go to a different school,
play different games in the street.
I'm not allowed to join.

I watch silently from my living room window
my own red ribbons trailing the top of the settee
as I wonder what the rules are
to the game I don't understand.

One day I come home from school to find
their car black and smoky
their window frames jagged
rooms empty
one light still on upstairs
smoke wisping out of the chimney
the air fume-dizzy
one ratty red ribbon
strewn across the step;

the area
    going
    downhill,

my own ribbon
a flame
on my neck.

Echo Chamber

This is why I hide
in my pretty chamber
with its polished walls and one-way mirrors.
I know
I'm not changing any minds
for all my poems and rants and fire
on a stage inside a concert hall
performing for the choir

but I step out into grass that's long and mucky
overgrown around my feet
and I hear their whispers on the wind:
I think she's trouble
There's more to that story.
What did she expect, walking through a park at night?
What did she expect, when she left the party drunk?
What did she expect What did she expect What did she expect

and those whispers wail like thunder
and I cover up my ears
and I race back to my chamber
and the thunder disappears

and I harmonise with those who sing like me,

incapable of agreeing to disagree
when unblocking my ears feels like
breaking in   two.

I stay –
and the reverberations tend my wounds.

I stay until the blood begins to scab.

Then I venture out
too soon
scratch off the surface
settle scrapes into scars
retreat. Rinse cuts with alcohol that stings my skin, repeat.

I'm not alone,
and we bandage each other
inflamed by fight.
We keep watch on moving shadows under doors,
tiptoeing towards daylight.

I know
we're not done trying.

Monster Hiding

for the 1 woman per week who is killed in Australia by a current/former partner

So they say we burn our bras
but they're setting us on fire
or they take us from our cars
and it's weekly, sometimes higher.

They invent the reasons why
we're not heard: because we're mad.
Ridicule us with a lie,
so they say we burn our bras.

Monster hiding in plain sight;
it can't be true, he's a good guy.
Or they insist she picked the fight.
They invent the reasons why.

They repeat, "It's not all men;
Don't walk alone; stay in at night."
But who is waiting in her bed?
Monster hiding in plain sight.

Whose voice matters, and whose doesn't
when the one they paint insane
is the voice that cries for justice?
They repeat, "It's not all men."

And it's weekly, sometimes higher,
monster hiding till he wasn't.
We no longer can deny
whose voice matters, and whose doesn't.

Stumbling Block

I've been buried
under layers of sweat-soaked cotton
padded tankinis, board shorts to my knees
expensive designs with hidden zips to feed

shriveling under fabric and flesh

hiding my home
explosive
poised to make men into monsters.

I can't focus
when you're wearing such a tight
grip on your power,
can't concentrate when I can see right through your
purity pledges, down to the cleavage
of behaviour and responsibility.

My voice falters on the phrase *wonderfully made*
while men are taught not to look directly
at this mantelpiece skeleton, heart plucked out
beating on the bench
for she will steal your soul.

Does God hide a light
for daring to sparkle

or would he have me sew my heart and   body
back together?

I'm not sure I can follow the shepherd
while hiding my   self
from the flock

and there it is.
My stumbling block.

**I take a break from editing poems and plans and choices, go to
the recycling centre**

where I like to watch the cans and bottles in the sorting machine,
all poured in from large, loud rubbish bags, queues of empty
drinks gathered dizzy after parties, tiny drops of yesterday still
caught inside, spinning and spinning in circles, like children
playing Ring-a-Ring-o-Rosie – *we all fall down* – back to try again,
joining the conveyor belt one at a time in careful lines, adjusting
adjusting adjusting until the machine has processed

every

last

one.

HIGHLIGHTER YELLOW

I don't miss
how small and silly I'd be
highlighter yellow staining your sensible grey
washing us both smaller
and smaller.

These days
I always choose a neon at the nail salon
I'm twenty beaded bracelets on each arm
jostling with bright letters
friendship quotes and pop music
the eyeliner flick
the lemon in the glass.

I read myself like a book
torch-lit under covers at midnight

and secretly, I bet there's a part of you thinking
Why couldn't she shine like that with me?

Strangers

Dusty book you once
dog-eared, now a silent shelf-
bound childhood favourite.

Language Barrier

I don't know how to talk to you
You're always changing the meaning of words

making *welcome* mean
hang mirrors where windows should be
squash bones and blood and flesh
wrap them in salt from stinging tears
tuck them quietly behind framed glass
where the image of God resides

defining *love* as
stoking the fires of hell on earth
to teach you my version
of heaven

insisting *compassion* means
biting you, then sucking out the venom
scorching your home and calling it a favour

pretending *believe* means
trampling the gut
silencing the heartbeat
self separating from self.

TROUBLEMAKER

The man who lives next door
holds open-air services around his barbecue;
his husband sings hymns of joy and love
to rival the psalms wisping out of stained-glass windows
on the steepled building he has never stepped inside.
He serves communion in long-necked bottles,
pealing tower bell muffled by the revelry.

Men behind lecterns always said
I should stand up for *the beliefs that make me who I am*
never set the thrum of my heart to the tempo around me

but when my heart quickens past the pace of Sunday's drums,
suddenly I'm not brave,
I'm a troublemaker
with itching ears and bleeding heart tuned
to the *perpetually offended*.

The beliefs that make me who I am
won't stand at the door crying *abomination!*
or offer an arms-spread-wide *welcome!* hinging on conditions
won't ignore trauma in the service of mission
or silence half the room in the name of tradition.
It's time for those inside the walls to learn to listen.

They say *that's a bit*
aggressive.

Stand up for your beliefs.
But not in a pulpit,

they say,
Don't tell men what to do –

that's a bit
progressive.

Tuck your protest under Sunday best,
hide reform under your pew.

Well here they are
spilling out from under hats and between hymn books:
the beliefs that make me who I am.
Justice, kindness, empathy, equality
recognising the image of God
in those outside the binary
or outside the boundary
in a man who loves a man
a woman who loves a woman
a child at a border separated from family

seeing the image of God
every time I see humanity

savouring the image of God
in the person who delivers my parcels
plastic Buddha on the dash
basking in the image of God
while gathered around
my neighbour's barbecue tongs and Beatles songs

finding the image of God
in the face of a woman

and refusing

to keep her

silent.

II

*You died, and I became a **ghost***

Another May ends and June descends like fog

The ocean wave   tumbles   settles

                                    bubbles over sand

                        subsides

leaves no trace behind
of strength that was; just my back story.
Another birthday passes.
To them, you're just a tide that never came back in
but I still see you everywhere.

Ghost

When you were ripped from me
I didn't know how to cry out.
The second stage of grief was not allowed.

All I knew was
there were shiny apples left over, unbobbed for in the bowl
and yesterday was Halloween
but today I was a ghost.

> I'd already shrunk small enough
> to fit in tiny spaces that I won't take up;
> a polished trophy
> *I must not interrupt*
> collecting dust,

waiting for a moment to disappear into.
Here it comes.

* * *

Each word dropped like shards of glass.
He isn't coming back.

My sliced-open skin began to bleed
and spurt and wither until I was empty
The dusty disc *skip skip repeat*
A ticking clock unplaiting soul and body

* * *

don't think i didn't notice
how my presence prickles skin and has them long for heat
don't think i didn't hear their screams
each time a tiny sob gasped out
an accidental spectral sound
don't think i didn't feel the warm breath of relief
as i floated high among the leaves
stayed quiet where i couldn't be seen
let cloudy head curl next to toes

you died
and i became a ghost

Christmas Without You

07-10-2007

It's 79 nights to Christmas. We always count from 100, but I forgot.

I wouldn't have forgotten
if you had been here to remind me.

Fanta and Coke

I remember tricky trinkets in Dublin joke shops
swirls of gold on navy carpeted hotel halls
crispy fish and chips from the place next door

I remember walks over cold sand dunes in Benone
Portstewart's rainbow windbreakers and sticky sunscreen limbs
tinny songs emerging from Barry's
the four of us swept along the sand
holding hands and jumping over waves
wind whipping paper windmills
knickerbocker glory
dripping
two   perfect
milky   rivers
down   my
chin

like raindrops on the window on our long drive to Cork at 4am
caravan rattling behind

I remember laps of the hotel pool in Coleraine,
swimming under you, not like the leisure centre in Carrick
where I knew just where to turn to avoid the deep end

I remember climbing the North Coast's high rocks
cheered on by family friends with braver eyes than mine

I remember late night walks back to our Wicklow tent
past the primary school's empty rooms
and crunchy summer grass

lip gloss free with magazines
smell of after-sun
sound of pages turning
white and purple wedding pictures
soccer ball bounce
blotchy dessert menus
tracking down a TV to watch the Williams sisters

I remember jukebox songs
same two favourites every time
alternating between a Fanta and a Coke
back when I could stomach the fizz

before autumn dawned harsh
before happy memories dried
like the paint on the ceiling in Windslow Drive;
I can't get back those pale pink hues
as dark evenings set in.

Once you were gone, you know
summer
just didn't dawn the same.

rip

There's a cut on the sole of my foot
from the day when the waves slammed and pulled

while my feet scraped in vain for solid ground
and desperate toes glanced off seaweeded rocks

                my mind dragged back
                    with the slowly building swell

crashed forward again, gasping breath plunged under,

                          body
                            pulled
                              out

neck craning in that   split-second   pause

hoping I'm kicking in the right direction
legs aching from fight

and again,   hand thrust high, beyond where I could see

and again   water curled behind me like a wall
                    holding me like a fist banged on the table

and again   fear swollen bigger than it's ever been

and again.

There's a shortness of breath when I see the ocean now.
I'm scared that next time I let the waves envelop me
I will plunge into that same wild surge   white foam panic
fill my lungs with salt and screams
scrape my feet against the slippery rocks
find nowhere solid beneath,
never try again,
miss the best chance I have
to   reach across death   grip my father's hand –

OUT OF BODY

I can't recall
a time when climbing made me tall
I only feel the brittle branch below
the slipping frame giving way
as my body makes
movements that I cannot trust

Exposure Therapy

Golden Shovel

I billow white sheets like unfurling waves over the bed I
made, brace myself with breaths I know
are too shallow, too small for this,
have sticky forest berry jam on dark toast I don't bother to cut,
fight against a young child's will
(the real one and the inner one I'm trying still to heal);
she whispers urgently, *Don't go*, I breathe my stomach big, but
butterflies are bigger; I whisper back, *You can trust me*, for I'm
you and you are fierce, though just two nights ago afraid,
I know in darkness with eyes thrown wide you still think of
that rising monster, that heaving betrayal; I will listen to what
you need as I approach the slamming waves, the
pounding heart, the stinging scar,
I promise; I will show you our strength, our power, our might
and I will make you proud of who you've grown to be.

I stayed home that night

working on my art homework, my papier-mâché fingers
draping uneven words on soggy cardboard limbs
paste dripping over the dark wood of the kitchen table
old black CD player in the corner, volume stuck on twenty-four
the song I wouldn't be able to listen to a decade after.
Don't let me be the last to know.

The phone sliced the night in two; before and after.
A turnstile at the railway station. No going back.
I asked how you were
but Mum avoided my question
I wonder if the shortbread noticed
half eaten on my plate, quarter batch still left in Tupperware
waiting for its chance to shine. *I'll be home soon* she said.

I rang Mum's boss to tell him she'd be late. *I'm so sorry Laura.*
Tone soft with sympathy – mistaken – I shook my head,
a disbelief he didn't see.
My Mum and Dad are on their way home.

Twenty-two years on, I hear that breath between the lines
and my scars glow hot like fresh burns
dread ignited with half-stories
abandoned biscuit crumbs falling
to the floor
ears straining for footsteps
around the corner.

The unturned stones are where the worries live.
The phone rings, and I have to answer it.

Mid-Air
23-11-2002: *the day that didn't exist*

I belong to no one
but those on either side of me
crammed close in airline seats

Time difference   skips   the hours   ahead
TearsBlurThemIntoOne.
Somehow we're not there yet.
No solid ground, no space to stretch, no cold blanket of sea;
only artificial air, as we hang in sky.

The engine's bluster
overpowers the dialogue
from the tiny chair-bound screen.
I push the volume higher
switch between channels
catch the end of *Serendipity* for the third time
Kate Beckinsale lying defeated on snow.

I've made this trip before
but that time I knew this quiet debt
would be repaid; I would return home.

This time
is the down-payment on a new life
and I'm forever out of pocket
out of place
out of sorts
 off   beat
having lived fewer hours than anyone else my age.

Please do not remove from aircraft.
Tucked in the seat in front
are diagrams and step-by-steps:
finding a life jacket
fitting an oxygen mask
escaping down a slide.
I wonder how many answers these cards might hold
For questions I have not thought to ask,
how many nights and days their line-drawn faces have spent
folded in a pocket,
how many tear-soaked travellers they have watched
bracing for impact.

I don't know this yet
but when I look back on yesterday
it will be the day I left
and when I look back on tomorrow
it will be the new in-breath
but when I look back on today
I will remember heavy, empty time
and fear.

Hours swell, contract, and disappear.

Storm in a Teacup

Eventually your gale subsides
and words I could have whispered
flood my mind, screaming like wind;
my teacup shakes in my hand, but I don't spill a drop.

In the Kitchen

Open the wooden slat blinds in the kitchen
tie back the curtains with the stenciled fruit
painted by your mum in red and green and yellow
Empty the vases of their thorny stalks
unbake the buns
lift the cheese from the top of the pasta bake
and seal it unopened in the fridge
stack the dishes clean at the back of dusty cupboards
turn on the CD player
un-know the ending
be thirteen again
dance

Transition

Not yet, they say
and laugh,
as waves build and crest
and fourth-day muscles shake to hold them back –

Reborn

The second time
I screamed
I yelled
I found my voice
my primal self;

I pulled you forth
with love and lung.

POLTERGEIST

I didn't notice for a long time

                                        till
                                        the
                                        furniture
                                        upturned

                                                                the lights
                                                              flicked off
                                                              and on

and off again

I wondered how long I had been stuck here

                              in eerie silence
                           touching purpled pain
                           hand straight through

                                                  didn't smack against it
                                             so couldn't feel the bruise

A removal van pulled up
full of questions
and anger unpacked its bags

                                                On stillest day,

                                                    the
                                                  windchimes
                                                  move

Cold air whistles through the door
A mirror shatters to the floor

                                        Crash

                              I looked around

                                        but
                              there was only
                                        me

This ghost wants to move on now
I had to set her

                    free

so I smudged sage through my home

salted the corners of my world with flavour I had buried
deep in the pantry

blessed the body I live in, felt it loosen and heal

I watched the other worlds dissolve in her eyes
heard her hum an old tune as she moved towards the light.
I whispered, *only you and I will ever understand
the fear and shame that pinned you here, haunting*

but I can feel your joyful spirit calling

as you move forward at last towards your rest.

III

You're the show I've had a ticket for
buried under clutter
and I'm the standing ovation
glowing write-up
spotlight
lover

September

I saw you on the train
or in the rain;
You're in a song or in the air
or in my skin or somewhere between the lines.
When the leaves began to fall
I waited for you to catch them
and turn them beautiful;
When he dawned like early spring, I tried to answer your
whispering trees.

Light

finds its way between
jagged edges, pouring in,
using every crack

Effervescence

Breathing shallow, goosebumps ready under skin;
everything I touch feels loud.
I might fall in love with the next stranger
whose eyes sweep over mine
might answer your next message with far too much detail
might walk in spring air, breeze-rippled hair and arms out wide
let sun pour light into my bones.
Everything I taste is warm
everything I say sounds loaded, flirty
familiar as home.
Inches apart, my skin lights up as if touched.
Say all the words I want. It's not enough.
This proliferative phase is drawing to a close.
Push your hands through my hair
like that September wind. Sing a song into my lungs.
Let daylight fall upon us intertwined.
Let me pull your body over mine.

**Seeing Through Your Eyes
Is Believing**

I'm the thump of the tree as it hits the forest floor
caught by the crisp autumn eiderdown

I'm the North Pole workshop
gift-wrapped in snow and powered by magic

I'm the live recording
the screamed lyric healing handheld hopes
the heartbreak hymn

(Sometimes I need to be *observed*
to feel real)

Lover

a slow piano intro
swapping secrets with another

sipped hot chocolate, smooth and creamy
foreign feel of fresh bedcovers

rhythmic tug of hair while braiding
watching waves unfold at sea

drumming rain on window pain

crescendo rise
sing harmony

I Found My People on a Fault Line

Shudder
settled in bones
but we ran to plant new
trees with tangled roots that hold me
steady.

Home

I miss the cliffs at Ballintoy
Portballintrae and Causeway Head
I miss the way the rough sea slams
and bounces off their rocky feet
I miss the jagged green and grey
the turquoise blue and foamy white
the crashing power and splashing height.

I miss the cold wind on my back
pushing me further down the Strand
the clinks and squeals of ice cream shops
and rollercoasters up ahead
I miss the paddling ice-numb toes
the cold Atlantic on my feet
run back to car, quick turn up heat.

I miss the town that's part of me
those narrow roads past fields of cows
the map I don't need to consult
for turns my muscle memory knows
the history held in castle walls
the main road edged by rocky beach
salt ocean air and shop-lined streets.

I miss the house, brushed brown and white
the neighbours' mirror image joined
I know that those who live there now
have changed the paint and added rooms

I miss the way our backyard stretched
my concert hall for summer plays
with friends roped in on sunny days.

I miss the day I walked in, found
you listening to Morning Mood
with your eyes closed, surrendered to
the swelling strings and heart and flute.
I miss the music shared with you
the foods you loved, your travel plans
sweet tooth, bike rides, the caravan
your jokes, your love for Portstewart Strand.

I miss the way those rugged cliffs
still sing your name; when all else shifts
I know they stand
while waves relentless push and smash and foam.
I miss the way you were my home.

Twenty-Three

Tomorrow we are married eleven years

Tonight I wore a leopard print corset and jeans
We ate pizza with prawns
licked salt and oil dripping from bread
under gilded pink sky

got drunk on twelve-dollar wine
next to waves
that howled like a belly laugh

feeling twenty-three again

Three

My stomach thinks we're   out   at   sea
poppy seed,   peppercorn,   blueberry,   feisty little raspberry

Little hiccups
            marking time
belly flutters
            tiny prize
prettiest of butterflies –

We'll never be two again
but three.

What a blessed thing to be.

Pastrami

Let's have curry tonight, you said.
Try and get things moving.

Walks uphill, stopping every ten minutes – seven – five.
1 – 2 – 3 – 4 – swell and crest and sweet release.
5 – 6 – 7 – 8 – overture to pas de deux.

Brace my body under seatbelt, radio volume like a shield.
I'll be there by this one's end.
1 – 2 – 3 – 4 – Vicious amber!
That wasn't five. It's four, it's three.
Park *stop* Lift *stop* Walk to reception desk *stop stop* Gown *stop* Bed
stop Please just *stop* sign *stop* here *stop stop*.
You're contracting a lot, she said. I knew.

Then breathe and gas and here-comes-another and gush and
stand and fall and scream and *I think I need to push* not yet not yet
and the anaesthetist isn't here, yes she is, too late, *push*.
B r e a t h e.
Push.

Him.

Dark blue eyes, slippery weight, tiny in my arms – *he's big* –
push once more
shaking
stitch
quick latch
incredulous
exhaustion

We'll name him in the morning.

Then midnight snack, pastrami sandwich
salve to spent and broken body
breathing soft and slow and peaceful
settle saturated senses

move to bedroom, gently sleep.

Remember when we used to go off-menu at Springsteens?

Bowl of chips from the sides menu please, shiny fried egg dip.
I'd pour water over ice to cool scorched tongue, wash
salt from lips; you'd order a coffee. You didn't mind
the double burn. Remember when I first moved out?
SOS calls halfway through recipes or disasters – You'd ask
for a photo then send the next step, the next step,
the next step. You've always been the extra arms, took more
heat, stood between me and slivers of glass. I've been so busy

being *theirs*; did I forget I'm *yours*? Band-Aids in my handbag
gone to waste, tangled in chip packets, folded between
Hot Wheels. My scraped knees weeping, waiting. The
bandage in your pocket. *SOS*. The next step: one foot
in front of the other, but this isn't a marathon. It's a contra dance.

Let's go out soon, just me and you –
order chips from the sides menu.

Coat

I wear this like a gorgeous vintage coat
that fits just slightly tight across the top
with antique-looking toggles to my throat.

The shoulders didn't grip me in the shop;
I only noticed beauty spanning years,
the way the sides fit loose, the knee-length drop.

The cosy hood is snug around my ears.
It blocks peripheral wind and joins me close
to those whose scent I still envisage here,

to other generations past, to those
I know have worn a coat like this before,
who've warmed in midnight colours, now a ghost.

But if I stay too long, I can no more
hold up my heavy arms around the ache;
I overheat; I drop it to the floor,

remember body curves under opaque.
It doesn't mean the coat is not for me.
Sometimes I'd like to find a way to make

it fit a little better, so I need
to hang it on the hook just while I breathe.

Guilty

Being angry already and it's 8am – Not getting on the floor and playing with you – Is it my fault that you struggle? – Is it a mistake I made already? – Oh, these stakes seem too high, darling – I am sure to mess it up – Will you still thrive if I am not always entertaining you – playing with you – enjoying you? – Sometimes I hide in the laundry – where I know exactly what to do – where a bleach soak never fails – hanging sleeves stroke my back until my tantrum fades – Will my choices still seem wise in one – ten – thirty years? – I yelled today – I watch my face reflected in the tumble dryer swirl – disgusted – Why doesn't this come naturally – like it did for my own mum? – I hear the volume rise and the cycle is complete – I push into the tumble and emerge, rinsed clean – Is it bedtime yet? I hate myself for wanting time for me. Was I too busy doing, forgetting just to be? Why won't you sleep? Why won't these lonely hours pass? Will I wish I had not wished them all away? Hours slip through tired fingers that strangle the voice inside – Berate myself for caving to an adult's wish – Vow next time I'll be your advocate – Morning brings a fresh stream of worry through my window – Did I put you in day care too early? – Should I have stayed home longer? – Why don't I have it in me? – I pull into the last space – Carry you inside – Why must you weep? Will you be fine in just one moment like they say – once I've walked away? I get back in the car – fear I might cry all day.

Fear of Heights

This sweet sugar high
comes down with a crash; I find
the space that I'm supposed to want
has lost all its appeal; eyes wild
I'm desperate to be reassured
when I'm not here, you're holding me in mind.

Fear pumps in my veins
twists around my family tree;
she has me singing party songs
but to the tune of elegies.
The lightest wind begins to shake
the acrophobic joy among her leaves.

Ricciolini

We go out for lunch, talk some more about
curly hair products.

Last night I tried a new restaurant.
I've been asking more questions,
striking up conversations, unbidden,
like six-year-old children –

I thought of you when I saw
full plates of tiny pasta curls

the way we spoke about leave-in conditioners with butterflies on
the label; how we both tuck away the tiny wisps that forget to curl,
shaped like olive leaves behind little ears; tiny spirals we've
begun to narrate in messages throughout work days; dancing on
the sauce at my birthday; stories that have twisted under skin;
little threads that bind these tales together; how our beliefs have
grown around our doubts like knots in wood –

and I wanted to message you
a photo of ricciolini.

Instead, I sent a message asking about your new shampoo
and did you want to meet for lunch?

It's not that I need to discuss hair care so much;
it's just that I'm really enjoying
having something
just for us.

Seven

Dancing tulle layers
skip with storybook magic;
I'll miss you like this.

I will not say
At least she's healthy.
If you need to speak of
how the licking flames burst you in two
and left you charred and scarred, forever marked
even though it feels like scratching my own scab
I will look your singed skin straight in the face. I will hold your melted hands between mine. I will not let you fade like glowing embers in the dirt while others fill their mouths with marshmallows they toasted in your warmth. I will watch you gather the ashes of your story and spread them for remembering.

– **Because the Mum Matters Too**

Wattle

I went back to that park
under canopy shade
where it began

tried to pin it
to the page

climbing on tree stumps
by spindly acacia trunks
rough bark under our palms
building sanctuaries of not-just-me
and wasn't-just-you

I sat on the swing
where I saw your scars
strode through the bark
we took home in our shoes
gum trees towering overhead
next to native shrubs with leaves like pins

rare and beautiful.

I left the swing swaying
in the still day
like proof

Jump

I like the moment
at the top
of the rollercoaster

or gasp of air mid-flight
before I touch
crisp blue water

or peering over the side
of the cliff
and jump

to
starexplodeconfettifall

that sacred   *p a u s e*

right
be
fore
I
lose
my
mind.

Shooting Star

I've never seen a shooting star
though I've spent evenings in dark backyards or rural cabins
in tents under moonlight
stars sprinkled like fairy bread
       like blinking eyes of commuting strangers
       like splatters of paint all flicked from the same brush

so close.

It was this I was waiting for.

           Fourteen in my Granda's greenhouse
        tomatoes squeezing juice between my fingers
and sycamores overhead, hearing how this move would ruin my life;
              sixteen, softening robust syllables;
               eighteen, alone in sleepover dark.

I learned to speak briefly, before their ears wander.
It was this, as I saw sisterhood from the outside
       stories of light dancing across black-soaked sky
       letters addressed to another
     glistening corps de ballet; my legs strained under my
     solo, ready for the wings.

It was this I was waiting for.

          You're the bookshop queue ahead of release
             you've read every word
             you're pressing for the sequel

My conversation slows and my accent creeps back.
It was this I was waiting for,

twenty-nine, gripping the relay baton, looking for my team.

I want to slip your names into conversation, tell who you are,
measure what each word weighs. You are the sparkly shoes. The
yellow highlighter. The buff and polish.

You've ruined me
for the dull, the unrequited, the superficial

– forever.

At the party tonight I spoke to everyone but you.

I suppose
  I'm just worried that I'll wear
out the fibres of your welcome,
      use up the dregs in the jars, slip past use-bys
        and leave the pantry
          a deflated balloon,
   burn the candles down to the end,

      wash dull and thin,
        a frayed old blanket,
  breed dust mites like a childhood teddy bear,
   a once-beloved novel,

     become the skinny jeans,
          the side part,
        the chunky highlights,
      the overplayed cassette tape ribbon

 fraying with words you used to know

      or perhaps it's a legacy
   from the drizzly-windowed Saturdays,
    the nights when cold wind
  nipped at summer, and loneliness

hovered
      in the doorway of the party

         like a ghost

Sundays

We did exactly what we were supposed to
with a three-strand cord, crocheted two moons around
one planet; so sure our solar system was the only one
that mattered. What a relief to find

that you were the sun, after all. That to choose each other
in every lifetime is just a more romantic way of saying
we choose each other again and again in this one; it's not
the multiverse we needed, but Sundays

with two glasses; two children on a swing set
is my church. A firepit, two marshmallows on a stick;
we unpicked, unravelled, pulled and pulled
till nothing remained but one long yarn

perfect to start something new
together; and what is a lifelong love
if not a continual picking and re-stringing,
fingers plucking well-versed harmonies

I've heard a hundred times before, fresh
by the firelight, a song I would not sing
at 23, earworm that won't be ignored now.
You say it's beautiful. A new scene taking shape

between our fingers. Stitches dropped and picked up,
explored and forgiven, and all the ways
you're not the boy I chose and I am
not that girl, and somehow you're still

everything I need; the story we wrote
as teens who knew everything
has come undone. I've broken promises
I never thought to speak out loud,

so implicit and relied-upon; but you still
lace your hand in mine. I think in the end
(or the middle; or this new beginning?)
we did exactly what we were supposed to.

BEACH

I love you most in ocean air
breeze washing into lungs
sand clung to toes, hat-rumpled hair
and salt droplets on tongues.

IV

*there's been a field for **wildflowers** out here all this time*

November

Sand not snow, pools not puddles
seasons muddled.
You can't come with me

but you're not a stamp in my passport
you're a citizenship
a keyring
a travel journal
a pocket watch
the silence between the notes.

Bilocation

When your heart b e a t s in another time zone
veins loop through narrow roads
you haven't seen in years
that split the endless green in two
your lungs inflate with North Coast winds
Atlantic salt trickles down cheeks
December snowballs roll through your belly
sweat drizzles like afternoon rain

fingers paint murals of bluebell woods
names are scribbled on the walls of your skin
and peace is precarious
wounds stitched closed each night
reopening with the sunrise
an organ high above the causeway
sends a refrain across the sea
that your ears can never unlearn,

when you wrap yourself in fields of patchwork
feel the sting of nettles pulsing under skin
skeleton shaped round rugged cliffs,

the drum-thump marches from your chest

and you have to wonder

how a heart can live outside bones so long.

Flower Season

Ever since that bouquet arrived, I've given myself permission.

I keep the vase filled till August turns to Christmas;
first your smiling daisy watches me remember.
Two weeks later, I choose freesias of every colour
the following week natives, strong and intricate.
I paint my house acacia yellow,
add new life as each bloom withers.

Not like those abandoned high in our kitchen
among traybakes and meringues
casserole dishes and Tupperware
books and bills pushed aside, kitchen table buried.
Week-old petals move from bench to floor
rotting scent among stale buns and dirty dishes
door opening and closing until finally
forgotten.

No, these flowers welcome me home
fluffy as meringues, but this time sweet-smelling and kind
open as a best friend's arms.
A wide pink rose roars my grief, nudges me to let go
for there are other hands here to catch her falling petals.
One dried out carnation pressed between pages
gently whispers
that my dates are worth the recording.

Nine years in
I celebrate my engagement party on his birthday
not telling anyone what the date means.

Tenth anniversary
I start a new job, *getting on with things.*
I thought grief should be silent.
Deep roots, baby buds.

Now it's been twenty-one. I've trimmed myself tiny.

These flowers let me
cut and water and display my heart.

Sea

I feel like me beside the sea.

Sometimes I pause before the yawning roar
                scared to dive beneath or let it sweep me flat;
                        summer feet protest the scorch
                                wriggle toes in prickly sand, run in,
lose footing as the bank gives way
                to valleys underwater
                        laugh as I resist the cold of ocean on my chest
throw my arms wide, squint into the sunshine
                let it bounce off limbs brown-patched with sand
                mesmerised by   constant   forward   motion
                        pushing wild waves over dusty land.
Perhaps it pulls me home to Carrickfergus
                childhood edges bound by ocean shores
                        castle keeping watch on ancient coastlines
                        walks on edge of town where water roars, or
perhaps it's tattooed in genes
                for I recall my father jumping over waves
                        and diving underwater
                                undeterred by wind
                                        or winter.
Gazing out to glittering stretch of water
                and letting waves unfold around my skin
                        pulls my soul to the surface
                                nudges my heart free –

I feel the most like me beside the sea.

What if I told you
I am bad?

Sparkle!

This theology is a bowl of shiny fruit,
crisp apples with one bite taken,
rotten inside.

Flowers on the windowsill lean towards the light
even if they never see the dark;
love is good news
even if you believe you deserve it.
Buds burst into colour,
sun warms my arms,
I bloom.

The seeds from which I grew
were crafted by the same hands
that poured the sparkle into seas
and set the glitter of the stars,
that shaped the tree trunk
and crisped each leaf
to fall,
that invited salt to tongues
painted raindrops into puddles
and danced soft breeze on December skin –
from this same heart, tumbled this tangle of rivers
this navy ink ocean
this tiny shoot, desperate for sunshine
for rainfall
for a field of flowers to grow in.

87

This creation is not evil, ugly, dark or demon.
She is summer.
She is nature, spice, sparkle,
wild and worthy.

Feet in the Dirt

God in my books has always been

father
sports coach
war hero
judge
king
master
lion

But my God is Mother God
feet firm in the dirt.
Divinity incarnate, skin-to-skin
deep-breathing life into the world
her body sacrificed
forever altered

and on day three,
though moods swing, chest aches
and tears perch ready for flowing,
she still has strength to rise
and push stones away.

These cracked and bruised nipples, this torn tissue,
this identity stretch-branded with white-line tattoos,

this wrinkled husk where she grew new life
and shrank on its release.

This wild love, elastic when flesh isn't,

growing and changing and stretched but
never shattered.

She grips my hand safe on the first day of school
hugs me close in sickness
rocks and sings to me, sending lullabies
deep into the night while the world sleeps,
wakes before the sun
to do it all again

for Love is a mother
who never runs out

unfailing hope
daily Easter miracle

spent body rising from the dust
glorious resurrection.

Sunflowers

Several week old
sunflowers
lean wearily
out of
the flowerbed
withered
or just weathered
and still
stretching for sun.

This Year Our Love

This year our love turns nineteen, darling.
sun-soaked, lusty, flourishing,
succulent and evergreen;

still a young thing.

Wonder

Like the prodigal who's coming home
just for the holidays
I'd love to find some comfort in familiar
for a moment

in the chords and carols
yule cliches
ancient turns of phrase
before all the questions
before the wrestle to be honest
when the wreaths and trees and truths
were all as sturdy and as natural
as each other

but I wonder

if maybe new eyes
are exactly what I need
upon this ancient story

to see it with the wonder
of one who wonders
what it means.

Maybe I could be the wise one
who follows where the light is

and maybe just like Mary
I'll find something here to treasure.

Stretch Marks

I have scars
in the places
where I grew

where old ideas
gave way to new

where certainty
stretched thin
and firmly held absolutes
have been outgrown
this roaring tiger skin the proof

engraved by open space
and messy truths.

First angry red
like welts, where fury
replaced shame.
Now faded stripes
mark growing pains.

Daisies

Summer days, the rainbow paints the sky.
It slows me right down, filters, bends my gaze
through spectacle of multicoloured light
and promise, sunshine proud upon my face.
Sometimes I close my eyes, take a long breath,
remember how dyed-berry hair would spill
upon my shoulders, warming on my neck,
feeling more at home than nature will.
I hold my head up high, imagining
that each vermillion strand sparks bold like fire.
I dream about the changes life will bring,
the twilight welcomed by cicada choir.
      The rainbow steeple hears my silent prayer;
      a thousand daisies tangle in my hair.

I am careful colours
arranged in flower bed,
pruned to gardener's vision,
expected to flower in season,
nourished, fruitful, perfect, even;
wilting, to flower again
or snipped for vases
to be propped
up by
still
water.
He
works
in
sweat
of
midday
sun,
trimming,
watering,
never
done.
Can't leave me be, or I might climb and wind and wildfire-
spread, a tangled weed. So dig soil deep, place seeds, fertilise;
shade carefully from scorching skies. Carefully correct, correct,
correct, perfect. Curate meticulously; design what ought to be.

well i want to be a wildflower

untended

growing

free

ACKNOWLEDGEMENTS

I acknowledge the Dharawal people, on whose unceded land I live, write and share stories.

There are many people whose support has made this book possible and I'm incredibly grateful. A huge thank you to:

Laurie Bolger for your thoughtful edits, your advice about publishing, your enthusiasm about my writing, your workshops and prompts, and for always reminding me to overload with sensation rather than information.

Amanda Dzimianski for your editor-eyes that see things I don't, for connecting with the spiritual questioning in these poems, and for the improvements you made to so many of them.

Bethany Tara Photography for always understanding my vision and turning it into art.

Counting Dead Women Australia, a project of Destroy the Joint, whose research was helpful in writing *Monster Hiding* and whose work is critical in raising awareness of violence against women.

The poets whose work made me excited about poetry, and made me think maybe I could do this too: most notably Kaitlin Shetler and Hollie McNish.

The teachers who built my confidence, especially Wendy Croger (for believing in my writing and remembering it after all these years), Stephen Lyons (for saying my name would be on the cover of a book one day – you were right!), and Rosemary McFarland (for choosing me to enter my first poetry reciting competition even though I was the shyest six-year-old in the class and *not* the obvious choice).

Family and friends who have been my muses, prompts, encouragers and editors.

Especially:

Bethany (for brainstorming creative ideas with me, and giving me a safe place to be authentic – even when that means I write poems about you and read them to your face. I couldn't stop writing us even if I wanted to); Rose, Lauren and Caitlin (for always wanting to read the uncensored version, and making me feel like I have nothing to hide and something worthwhile to share. What a gift you are); Alice (for your insights into the world of publishing, your generous answers to my many questions, and your wise words when I worried about who might read my soul on these pages. I couldn't have done this without you); Gill (for sharing your own work with me – your creativity and encouragement are inspiring); Meg (for your helpful feedback, and teaching me new poetry forms); Andrew (for sharing my scars, and my Fanta-and-Coke summers); Dave (for making poetry a staple of our home); and Simon (for normalising questions).

Mum, for passing on a love of reading and writing, and for demonstrating the most selfless version of motherhood.

Madeline and Theodore, for your curiosity, kindness, creativity and humour. Your love has made my life bigger.

Joshua, for loving me in all my poems and rants and fire, believing in me relentlessly, and always being on my team. I can't sum it up in one line, so I've done my best with numerous love poems and a book dedication. This year our love is 22… still a young thing x

Dad, for everything you gave me in the 13 years we had, for inspiring a love of the ocean and for teaching me to listen to music with my eyes closed.

And you, the reader – for caring about my words and bearing witness to these experiences. This book is the thump of the tree falling in the forest and because of you, it's real.

PREVIOUSLY PUBLISHED WORK

Lost, Stretch Marks and *wildflower* were previously published in *Cothumos.*

I Stayed Home That Night was previously published in *Sad Girl Diaries.*

Earlier versions of *Ghost, In The Kitchen, Poltergeist, Home, September, November* and *May* were previously published in *Missing Pieces: Poetry and Prose,* an anthology by Quillkeepers Press.

Flower Season was previously published in *The Chariot Press Literary Journal.*

Red Ribbon was previously published by *Pine Row.*

Good Friday Agreement was previously published in *Chaos, Crisis, Conflict,* an anthology by the Moonstone Arts Centre.

At the party tonight, I spoke to everyone but you was longlisted for the Anthology Poetry Competition 2024.

ABOUT THE AUTHOR

Laura grew up in Carrickfergus, Northern Ireland, and moved to Australia when she was fifteen. She lives on Dharawal land with her husband Joshua and their two children.

Laura was a Sydney finalist at the Australian Poetry Slam in both 2023 and 2025. She is also a songwriter and has played her original songs in many venues around Sydney. Laura studied social science and psychology at Western Sydney University, and has worked for the past 16 years as a psychologist. She considers creative writing to be just as important as therapy when it comes to self-care and meaning-making (although she believes everyone should try both).

Laura's first publication was a poem called *Baby Moses* when she was eleven years old. Her more recent publications include *The Chariot Press Literary Journal, Griffel,* and a selection of five poems published in *Missing Pieces,* an anthology on grief published by Quillkeepers Press in 2024. This is her first full-length collection.

You can find Laura's poetry on Instagram and TikTok @Poems.by.Laura and can sign up to her mailing list or find more of her work here:

Photo by Bethany Tara Photography

www.ingramcontent.com/pod-product-compliance
Lightning Source LLC
Chambersburg PA
CBHW011936050726
47590CB00011B/3313